MW01228302

Rescued Daughter

Stacey Winns

TYMM PUBLISHING

Tymm Publishing Services

Rescued Daughter

Copyright © 2023 by Stacey Winns

Editing: Felicia Murrell

Publishing Assistance: Tyora Moody, TymmPublishing.com

Contents

Dedication

I dedicate this book to my family. Thank you for everything.

This book is also dedicated to those who are sick and suffering in their addiction and identity. God is not a far from you; you too will be rescued.

Acknowledgements

To Denise A. Kelley, for believing in my gift and helping to bring it out. Zack and Beth Bib, for all your support and giving me a platform to share God's word and hope of recovery. My church, The Journey, for being a big part of my healing process. SIR, for walking with me in my recovery and the women of SIR women's bible study, you ladies rock. I love you!

Chapter One

False Identity

There I was, locked up in the county jail in Colorado Springs, charged with third degree assault. I reeked of alcohol and all I wanted to do was sleep. Booked, fingerprinted, mugshot taken, I received my orange jumpsuit with the matching flip flops and was escorted to my cell. I jumped on the top bunk and passed out for the night.

I awakened to a guard calling somebody's name, when I opened my eyes and sat up, I found myself surrounded by more women dressed in orange. My mouth was pasty, and I had the worst headache ever. The holding block was so bright, I squinted my eyes almost completely shut. I could barely see. I vaguely remembered what happened, then I reached up and put my hand on the back of my head. Feeling the big, tender knot, it all came flooding back.

Our relationship was nothing short of destructive, but I never thought it would get this far. Our addiction had gotten the best of both of us. It seemed like we were drinking and arguing all day. I threatened to pack my bags and leave but that made things worse, escalating the argument.

I decided to take a walk and cool down. As I was about to go out the door, she charged at me with an iron and busted me in the back of my head. The next thing I knew we were in a fight for dominance. I found myself on top of her. Yes, HER. I was about to strike a blow, defend myself against her rage. I realized what was happening; I couldn't believe I was in this kind of situation.

As I released her, I heard a loud *bam*. I turned towards the front door and her sister Vicky was breaking in the door. Everything seemed to be happening in slow motion. Vicky ran over and grabbed me, while Bre slid up against the wall. After Vicky released me, she ran to help her sister. I stood there shaking; it felt like I was in a nightmare.

The next thing I knew, the police arrived, and I was carried down to the jail in handcuffs. The back of the cop car was so tight, my knees were up against my chest and my wrist hurt from the cuffs.

Something took hold of me that day. I was not myself at all. I sat on that bunk asking myself what happened to my life? What was I doing in Colorado Springs where I knew nobody but the two people that had me locked up? Somewhere in my life, I had developed a false sense of identity. I didn't know who I was or who God intended for me to be.

Sometimes experiences in life shape us into something we were never meant to be and the evil deeds of others can leave an indelible mark on our soul for a long time. This is my story of the rescuing hand of God in my life. I pray that you, the reader, will be blessed through my journey.

Chapter Two

Sweet Memories

1973

The adventure would start in the morning, and my sister and my six-year-old self could not wait. Summertime was here and like every other summer before this one, we stayed up all night talking about what we would do when we got there. My mother sent me and my sister down south on the Greyhound bus to spend the summer at Grandma Ethel's house.

Summer was a chance to cut loose and absorb all the benefits of the South. Running free, barefoot and all, I had all the dirt from outside on my face, hands and feet and didn't even get yelled at.

One summer, my cousins Andre and Vincent challenged me to climb the big old tree in front of Grandma's house. They didn't know I was a pro at climbing the monkey bars during free time at school up north, so I was up to the challenge.

I reached down into the dirt that surrounded the trees. As I rubbed it into my hands, my cousin, Big Stacey yelled, "Grandma, Stacey getting ready to climb that tree in the front. She's going to fall and break her neck!"

I yelled back, "No I'm not. I can do it, watch!" I jumped up on that tree like a cat and froze. Looking up, I became dizzy. This tree was gigantic. It was the biggest tree out there and nobody had ever attempted to climb it.

I held on to the tree and looked up. The branches seemed so far away, but I remember thinking, *you can do it, you can climb it*. So, with my feet and hands, I started scaling upwards. My cousins were chanting, "Climb! Climb! Climb!"

During all that chanting, there was a big *BOOM!* And there was Grandma busting through that screen door, apron on and hands on her hip, yelling, "Chile, get yourself off that tree. You know girls don't climb trees!"

I felt those big hands wrap around my little waist and take me down off the tree. I shouted, "But, Grandma, I can do it. You're not giving me a chance to do it."

Grandma said in her southern accent, "Chile, if God wanted you to climb trees, he would have made you a monkey. Now get yourself on that porch and sit for a little while."

With my face turned up and arms folded, I stomped up those stairs and sat on the top step.

Grandma didn't appreciate that much. "And don't be stomping around here and fix your face for it stay like that," she said.

So, I did what she said. But that big old tree stood as a symbol of how I never got to conquer what I knew I could after somebody decided to tell me that I couldn't.

I sat on the porch for a while, and then it was time to go apple picking. I loved going apple picking, especially on Saturdays. Grandma would make an apple pie or cook those apples into something delicious on Sunday morning, and that alone got me excited.

After apple picking, we played a game of horseshoe. My cousins didn't like to play horseshoe with me. When I lost, I'd get mad and start running around threatening to hit everybody. I get tickled thinking about it. It happened all the time. I don't know why I played. The horseshoe was too heavy for me to throw, and I knew I would lose.

After a day of trying to conquer that tree, apple picking, chasing my cousins and running wild, we had to settle in and get ready for bed. Grandma had this big tin tub that everybody had to bathe in. She used a touch of bleach in the water and by the time she was done, it felt like I had the black scrubbed right off me.

My cousins and I slept on pallets on the floor. There were around twelve of us altogether, but I really didn't mind. I loved sleeping on those pallets. Grandma's multicolored quilts smelled so fresh after she took them off the clothesline. I wrapped my whole body up in them and drifted off into dreamland, not a care in the whole world.

RESCUED DAUGHTER

On Sunday morning, the smell of breakfast cooking in the kitchen filled the air while my cousin Ronald played gospel hymns on the old piano in the living room. The sound of Grandma humming sounded sweet to my ears.

That aroma from the kitchen hit my nose and my eyes popped wide open. I could hear the bacon sizzling, and I got up to see those apples cooking in the cast iron pan. Grandma was scrambling eggs with the wooden spoon she used to threaten to spank our butts with when we misbehaved.

I watched her butter homemade biscuits. The whole time, she was humming those hymns. The entire kitchen burst with nothing but flavor, and I stood there feeling safe and loved.

After a few minutes, the house started to awaken, and the hustle and bustle began. Everyone ran to the kitchen table ready to eat. But the table wasn't exactly big enough for everyone, so we shoved each other for more space. At first glance, it might not have looked like it, but there was nothing but love at that table.

My grandmother's sister was living with her at the time. Mern Carter, that's what we called her, was mentally challenged. I wasn't sure if she was born that way or if something happened. But she was right there at the table stuffing her mouth with food like everybody else.

Mern reminded me of an oversized kid. I played with her and whenever I needed a hug, besides going to Grandma, I went to Mern and she would sit me on her lap and give me the biggest hug, rubbing her cheek against mine.

It was like feeding an army at that kitchen table, but we always cleaned our plates. Afterwards, the oldest girls washed the dishes and cleaned the kitchen. Getting ready for church was an event all by itself. My sister helped me get dressed, but Grandma fixed my hair. I hated getting my hair straightened with the straightening comb. I remember that thick grease in the red or blue jar with the name "Crown" on it in big white letters. I remember having burn marks on my neck or the tip of my ear. To top it all off, I had to walk around with different color barrettes dangling from my short braids.

When everyone was ready, Grandma lined us up at the front door like we were cars coming off the assembly line for a final inspection. Grandma owned a big yellow bus. To this day, I have no idea where she got that bus. Maybe she worked for the school system, I'm not exactly sure.

I loved riding in that school bus. Riding on it was like an adventure and going down that winding country road with all the hills was like being on a roller coaster. I would lift my hands and yell, "Whee," every time the bus went down one of those steep hills. Then I would yell, "Do it again, Grandma, do it again!"

By the time we pulled up at the church, my dress was bunched up from all the moving around. Coming off the bus, Grandma stopped me. "Hold on, chile," she said. She straightened my dress with the frilly lace and wiped off my patent leather shoes. After fixing my little white socks, she shook her head and said, "Just a mess."

We marched behind Grandma like she was Sarge and we were her troops. "One, two, three, four." The mothers of the church would say, "There's Mother Ethel and her babies."

I always smiled when I heard that. I was proud to be one of Grandma's babies. Summertime at Grandma's was the best time.

I had a good sense of who I was, a sense of identity. I was the granddaughter of Ethel Osborne, an innocent six-year-old little girl. I wanted those good times to last forever and a day, but now they are wonderful memories. Oh, how I miss those times. As I reminisce throughout these pages, my heart smiles sharing these times of joy with you.

Sometime later, my life would change in an unexpected and traumatic way. But that little playful girl who loved to climb trees would be protected through it all. God kept her safe deep down inside of me and, by the grace of God, she would emerge as the woman God intended for her to become all along.

Chapter Three

The Violation

1980

I was doing a semester in Virginia at Langston Junior High School. I was thirteen years old, the first time I was raped. My uncle's friend violated me. That experience dramatically changed my life and the way I saw all men.

I was walking to my granddad's house when he pulled up in his yellow Cadillac with the black top. He smiled and said, "Where you headed?"

"To my granddad's," I said.

"Hop in, I'll take you."

He was my uncle's friend. I didn't think anything of it. I thought he was being nice, and I trusted his smile.

One of those scented things dangled from the mirror made the car smelled good inside. The yellow seats smelled like new leather; I loved that new car smell. The black floormats had the words "Cadillac" written in yellow. It was the sharpest ride my thirteen-year-old self had ever seen.

Chuck was dressed in a black and white terry cloth sweatsuit with a pair of clean white Adidas sneakers with the black stripes on the side. He had a thin gold chain around his neck and an earring in his left ear. Whenever I saw him with my uncle, he was always nice to me. He'd smile and say, "Hey, Stace."

People always cut my name short, leaving off the "y," but I didn't mind.

One of my favorite rap songs, Curtis Blow's "The Breaks," was playing on the radio. I strapped myself in and sat back, jamming to the music.

He said, "So, Stace, how old are you?"

"Thirteen."

"Oh, ok. What grade is that?"

14

"Eighth."

"Oh, ok. You're practically grown then."

I laughed a little and said, "Nahh, I'm not grown. I still have a few more years to go. You should know that."

With a side smile, he said, "I know, I know. I'm messing with you. I need to pick something up from my aunt's house, ok?"

I was chilling and jamming, so I didn't mind. "Ok," I said.

When we got to his aunt's house, he got out the car, bent down and brushed off one of his sneakers. "Be right back," he said.

I waited in the car and when he came back, he said, "I need to drop something off at a friend's house. You wanna come with me?"

"Ok, but after that I have to get home."

When we drove off, he pulled out a bag of weed, threw it in my lap. "You know how to roll up?" he asked.

I said confidently, "Yep, I sure do."

I noticed he was driving quite a distance. We were in the part called 360, that's the country. So, I asked. "How much further?"

"We're almost there," he said.

But something didn't feel right.

He pulled up at this house and there appeared to be nobody home. It didn't even seem like anybody lived there. The area had nothing but woods. I couldn't see the road anymore. He stopped the car and turned off the music. He was staring at me, and then in a calm voice, he said, "Get in the back."

I didn't understand. I was confused. "But isn't this your friend's house? Why do you want me to get in the back?"

"If you don't get back there, I'm going to leave you out here and you'll have to walk home with these animals picking up your scent." The anger in his voice shook me to my core. He shouted, "Now get back there!!"

I was so scared; I didn't know what to do. My thoughts were racing. It was almost getting dark. If I died out there, nobody would know. So, I did what he said.

After I went to the back seat, he came back there and grabbed me. I wasn't strong enough. All I could do was let him do what he wanted to do.

I wanted to scream but nothing came out. I lay there and cried until he was done.

When he got up off me, he stood outside the car looking at me. After a few seconds, he said, "Get out!" I slid out and pulled up my pants with tears pouring down my face. He took his hand and wiped my tears and closed the back door. Then he walked over to the driver's side of the car and got in, cranked the car up and drove off. He was going to leave me anyway.

As if he'd changed his mind, the car came to a complete halt, and he reached over to the passenger's side. After opening the door, he sat there waiting for me to get in. Still fixing my clothes, I walked slowly over to the car and got in. I dared not look at him. Neither one of us said a word as he drove me home.

He dropped me off and drove away. I stood there looking at my granddad's house, but I didn't want to go in. I was ashamed. I didn't want anybody to see me in that condition and ask what happened.

My granddad lived across the street from a graveyard, and I remember thinking *I'm going to take this to my grave.* I wanted to die right then and there. I didn't want to live with the shame of this following me for the rest of my life.

A few years ago, I heard that our bodies record what happens to it. I'm sure my body recorded that assault, and that I spent years in torment afterwards.

When the semester was over, I moved back to New York with my mother. After that experience, I was overpowered by so much self-hatred, I did everything I could to destroy myself. I felt like I was dead emotionally and spiritually. The pain was so overwhelming at times, I wanted to die altogether. I didn't want to live the rest of my life in an unbearable pit of pain, but I wasn't sure if there would be any hope, any light at the end of this dark tunnel.

Chapter Four

Lost Sheep

1982

I began to live my whole life in a dream-like state. There wasn't a moment that went by where I wasn't high off something or intoxicated off whatever I could get my hands on to drink. I couldn't breathe when I was at home, so I ran the streets constantly.

I was still holding on to my secret. I tucked it deep down inside, numbing the pain as much as I could to the point of becoming suicidal. One morning, my baby sister and I were getting ready for school. We got into an argument about the bathroom sink not being cleaned after I used it. I became so angry; I was yelling at the top of my voice. My whole body was shaking; my eyes became big. Something so minor had set me off.

Anytime the feeling of shame peeked its ugly head, I became enraged. I felt degraded. That particular morning, I turned to the wall in the hallway by the bathroom and punched two holes in it. Then, without even thinking, as if something was controlling my body, I ran to the terrace, busted the door open and took a flying leap. The next thing I knew, I was on the other side of the terrace.

My mother somehow got a hold of the hood on my hoodie and wrapped it around her hand. She was holding on to it so tight, she was choking me. She was able to get me back on the safe side of the terrace and pull me back into the house. At this point, 9-1-1 had to be called.

By the time the police came, everything had calmed down and we were sitting in the living room. The officers were two of the biggest cops I had ever seen, so I definitely made sure I was chill.

They came in with their creased pants, shiny badges and serious looks on their faces. They sat down with me and my mom to get the story about what was happening. One of them turned to me after finding out about my suicide attempt and asked, "What is so wrong that you would do that? What's going on?"

I couldn't say a word. I sat there looking down and fiddling with the string on my hoodie. I was ashamed, embarrassed. I felt like I had no voice. I was screaming on the inside, but my voice would not speak; I was silent.

Since everything appeared to have calmed down and I appeared to them to be alright, the intervention ended and the two nice officers took their leave after saying to me, "You behave yourself now and stop giving your mother grief."

It was around 8:00 a.m. and instead of going to my school, I went to my homegirl's school to see if she had arrived. The plan was to skip school and go to our spot. Sure enough, Gayle was hanging out across the street smoking a big fat joint.

Gayle was unique. Her clothes never matched, but she always had on the latest gear, and she had ponytails all over her head with rubber bands in different colors. She was a character, but I thought she was different and cool. I liked her from the first day we met on the basketball court.

I walked up to her and said, "Let me hit that," and she immediately passed the joint to me. She noticed the scratch on my neck. "Yo, what happened to you?"

I shrugged. "Nothing, I was attempting to fly and my mom's got in the way."

Gayle paused and looked at me for a minute with this serious look. Then she said, "Oh, aight," and we both chuckled a little.

It was almost time for the bell to ring for homeroom. If you got checked in for homeroom, you pretty much were considered checked in for the whole day. So, Gayle went to homeroom, and I waited for her at the side entrance of the school. When she came out, we headed for our spot.

We were chilling at the weed spot when this dude, Mike, pulled out some of this white powder in a twenty-dollar bill. "Y'all ever had any of this?" he asked.

We were like, "What's that?"

"This the big joint right here," Mike said. He put some weed in some bamboo paper and sprinkled some of the white powder on top of the weed before rolling it up. When he lit it, it smelled funny, like alcohol.

He handed it to me, and I took a big toke. He was like, "Easy with it now." My whole body felt tingly. I closed my eyes and it felt like I was flying. I felt my heart beating a little faster and I could taste the cocaine in the back of my throat and on my lips. I felt adrenaline all over my body. It was the best feeling in the world. I was hooked.

He was smiling. "You like that, huh?"

Almost choking, I said, "Hell yeah."

"That's that coke. If y'all ever wanna buy some, come to me. Don't go nowhere else, aight?"

I was like, "Bet."

Gayle and I spent the rest of the day at the spot getting high while Mike did his job selling weed through the peephole in the door.

A few months later, I was hanging with some people in my neighborhood. We were in the exit of the projects getting high. We noticed we were almost done with the weed, so Lester, who was the cousin of a mutual friend, said he would go get some more. He turned to me and said, "You down to come with me?"

I said ok and we walked two blocks over from the projects to Chester Avenue.

We entered the building's elevator and Lester put on his shades. They were reflective, the kind of shades that I could see myself in. I thought putting on shades was a little strange since it was already dark and there was no sun whatsoever in the elevator.

He cut a wicked smile. "You aight?" he asked.

"Yeah, I'm ok," I said.

"Aight. Just checking, you look high as hell."

I gave a little smile. "I am," I said.

"Yeah, me too," he said.

I figured that was the reason he put on his shades.

At his apartment, he put his key in the door and opened it. Instead of going in, he motioned for me to go in before him. I thought he was being polite, but it was really so that he could go in last and lock the door behind him. I turned around when I heard the door lock. "Why are you locking the door? We're going right back out."

"Give me a minute," he said, "let me go to the bathroom first." He went to the back, and I sat down in the living room looking around. I was admiring the posters of Doug E. Fresh and the Get Fresh Crew and Run DMC on the walls.

When he came out, I immediately noticed his zipper was opened. I also noticed the big bag of weed in his hand. He sat the weed on the table and started rolling up a joint. I watched, but I was beginning to feel nervous. I could feel the hairs stand up on the back of my neck. I looked around the room, and I swear I heard a voice in my head say, *Go home.* When I stood, he snatched my arm and made me sit back down. "Don't be in such a rush. Why are you rushing?"

"We came to get the weed. Let's get back to everybody."

"Nahhh, let's chill here for a few." After rolling the joint, he lit it and leaned all the way back.

"You like me, don't you?" Looking down at himself, he said, "You like this, right?"

"No, I think we need to go. Come on, let's go."

"You telling me you don't like this? You gay?"

I looked at him and he slowly sat back up and put the joint into the ashtray. Before I knew it, he grabbed me and got on top of me. Holding my arms tight behind my head, he pressed himself on me, to the point I couldn't move.

With me pinned down, in a deep wicked voice through clenched teeth, he said, "If you don't give it to me, Imma release my dogs on you. Imma sic 'em on you."

I could hear the dogs moving and barking in the back. I knew he wasn't lying and that he'd really do it.

This time, the voice in my head was telling me to fight, but my body wouldn't do what the voice was saying. As with Chuck, I lay there. But this time, I didn't cry. I could feel Lester's breath hot on my neck. His body was so heavy, he was almost smothering me. I wanted him to hurry up and finish before I passed out.

At this point, I wasn't even present in my mind. I was thinking about my grandmother's house, running around with my cousins. I could hear our laughter. I wasn't even aware of how long it was taking him. When he was done, I felt his body move off mine. With sweat dripping off his face, he sat up and zipped up his pants. Then he lit the joint again and leaned back on the sofa.

I think he killed all normal emotions I had. I could feel nothing afterward. When I decided to sit up and pull my pants up and adjust the rest of my clothes, he grabbed the back of my neck and squeezed. "You tell anybody and I'll hurt you. You know I'll do it, right?"

All I could do was shake my head yes. He slapped the back of my neck and said, "Good, let's go."

I didn't go back with him to the exit where everybody was waiting for us. I went home instead. That night, I decided from now on I would give it up. No one would have to take it; my body was for whoever wanted it. I figured this was all I was good for. I was soiled, dirty, damaged goods.

This was what my life would be like. I wasn't a treasure or special. I was nothing. Nothing at all.

Chapter Five

The Big Scare

1984

At sixteen years old, my mom decided to send me to the Job Corps in Charleston, West Virginia. She thought that if I got out of the neighborhood, I would be alright. But there's a saying that seems to hold true, "Wherever you go, there you are." Sending me away wasn't going to fix what was wrong. Everything I got in New York, I was able to get in Charleston and then some.

By this time, crack had come on the scene, and I was using a little bit of this and a little bit of that. Pills like Quaaludes and Black Beauties. There was this liquid stuff called Locker Room, which came in a brown bottle. When you sniffed it, everything went black and, in that moment, you would not know what was going on around you. That's how much I didn't care what happened to me.

Charleston was also the place where I had my first relationship with a female. I didn't want to have anything to do with men. I feared them and I didn't trust any of them. I became a totally different person in Job Corps.

I didn't even want to be a female anymore. I wanted to be a dominant individual that would never be taken advantage of again. So, I created this dominant persona, a more masculine persona. This persona made me feel safer and more in control of my own body.

I turned my attention towards females. I wasn't threatened by them. I wouldn't be violated by them. I wouldn't be harmed by them. And although there was a part of me that knew this was not who I was, this wasn't the design of God for my life, I couldn't stomach guys at this point. I would spend many years, off and on, in relationships with females. I didn't care not one bit.

I thought being with women was the answer. I realize now that it was another way I punished myself.

When I was done with Job Corps, I went back home to New York. At home, crack was ten times as bad on the streets as it was in Charleston. It had devastated my community.

People that I went to school with and hung out with looked like they went through the *Twilight Zone*, but in no way did that deter me.

One day, me and a friend who lived in my building hung out all day smoking weed, crack, drinking, even popping acid called Purple Mescaline. For some reason, that night we decided to go to the movies and that's when the night turned interesting.

While sitting in the movie theater, I began to trip. It was like the people on the screen were so close to my face I could reach out and touch them and this was not a three-dimensional movie.

My heart started beating so fast it felt like it was going to burst right out of my chest. I jumped out of my seat and ran out of there so fast that I ran into a parked car and laid on top of the hood.

Tee ran out behind me. "What's wrong, Stace?"

I held my chest. Still breathing hard, I said, "My heart is going to stop tonight. I'm about to die."

Tee hailed a cab, and we rode home. When we got to my door, Tee didn't bother ringing the doorbell, she jetted into the exit and ran down the stairs.

Thank God I had my key. I opened the door quietly. I could hear my mom in the kitchen cooking, so I eased myself to my bedroom and closed the door. It was so quiet in the room I could hear my heartbeat. It was ready to beat right out of my chest like the police beating down a suspect's door.

I couldn't breathe. I started sweating. I sat up quickly and I just knew that my heart was going to stop.

I decided to go tell my mom what was happening. My mother had every right to be fed up with me. I had put her through so much and she was at the end of her rope.

When I finally told her what was going on, she turned to me and said, "Now, I told you about being out there messing with that stuff. It's nothing more I can do for you."

She still had no idea of the pain I was in. After all these years, I was still holding on to and trying to bury all that had happened to me.

I didn't understand how to process or deal with my trauma. The only thing I knew to do was try my best to numb the pain and destroy myself in the process.

Mom went to the back and came out with twenty dollars. She told me to take myself to the hospital.

For the first time, I realized that I didn't want to die. I said "But, Ma, I can't go alone. Not like this."

My eldest sister was visiting from Texas. She came through the door and immediately recognized that something was wrong. "What's wrong with you?" she asked.

"I'm going to die tonight," I told her.

I was so glad she agreed to take me to the hospital. Once I got there, I ran inside. Like, I literally ran and hit my knees, slid across the floor like James Brown and cried out for someone to help me.

The nurses came and put me in a room. The doctor came in to examine me. When he realized I was high, he asked me what I had taken.

I told him and he gave me some kind of shot and everything started to settle down and my heart began beating normal. After a couple of hours of observation, I was allowed to leave.

That entire weekend, I refused to go out and see anybody. I thought I wanted to kill myself, die a slow death. But that night, when I literally thought death was knocking on my door, when I thought, I was going to breathe my last breath, I realized I didn't want to die at all.

There is something about thinking that your heart is going to stop that scares you straight and causes you to see things from a whole different perspective. I started going back to church with my mother and even took up a bible study with a woman from our former place of worship.

My life began to transform, and I realized that I needed Jesus. I was desperately trying to stay as close to him as I possibly could.

I even got into ministry, doing outreach and street evangelism. I spent the next several years of my life trying to please God and live for him.

I ended up getting married. I stayed married for four years and then my past grabbed ahold of me. I thought I was healed, but I wasn't. I ended up reverting back to my old habits and life. That false identity wouldn't turn me loose no matter the work I tried to do for God, no matter how much I tried to pay it back for all that I had done.

When I relapsed back into my addiction and that lifestyle I hated so much, I certainly didn't think I would make it back, at least not in my right mind. All I have to say is, BUT GOD!

Chapter Six

Freedom

Sitting on that bunk in the Colorado Springs jail, I knew this would be a turning point. After looking back at the ugly things that had taken place in my life, it was time to look forward. I decided if I ever got out of jail, I would go back home to my family where I could start my life over again.

I had absolutely no idea how that was going to happen or what that would look like, but I knew it had to happen.

After being locked up for seventeen hours, the guard came that night and knocked on my cell "Winns! You've made bail. It's time to go home."

I was so relieved. I couldn't move fast enough to get out of there once and for all.

My family had called Bre and demanded that she post bail. They were gracious enough to send the funds for my release. I thought I was going to rot in that jail, but I walked out those doors free.

Seventeen hours felt like seventeen years. I thought to myself, *I'm a convict. This must be my bottom.* Perhaps it was a bit dramatic, but that was how I felt at the moment.

The next day while Bre was at work, I packed my clothes to head to the Greyhound bus station.

I wanted to clean up the house well before I left. I didn't want to leave any trace of myself there; I never wanted to look back.

I heard the key in the door before the doorknob turned. Then the door opened.

She'd gotten off early. My plan to leave while she was at work was completely ruined. She looked down at my suitcases and let out a sigh. "Where are you going?" she asked.

I told her it was time for me to go. I knew something bad was going to happen, something worse than spending seventeen hours in jail.

She stared at me and said, "So, you were going to leave just like that? Without saying bye to me?"

I told her that I thought it was for the best. She entered the house and closed the door, set her pocketbook on the couch. Then she went to the back room to change her clothes without saying another word to me.

I was nervous. Walking on eggshells, I eased my way through the house and finished dusting.

To my surprise, she was calm, a little too calm. After about thirty minutes of silence, she said, "Well, before you leave, can you go to the store and get some beer? Maybe we can drink together one last time. Can we at least do that?"

I obliged her. I didn't want things to go left; I wanted a smooth transition. I don't know why I thought alcohol was going to make that happen when past experiences said this was going to go left fast.

But I figured since my life was about to change, maybe this one last time would be alright.

We sat in the bedroom drinking and talking, even laughing, and before I knew it, the time had gotten away from us.

I decided to take a later bus since I missed the one I was supposed to take and checked to see when the next bus was leaving.

She thought this time together would change my mind and I would stay. But it didn't change anything. I was still leaving.

At 9:30 p.m., I picked up the phone to call a cab.

"What are you doing?" she asked.

"Calling a cab."

"For what?"

"To take me to the bus station."

"You're still leaving?"

"Yeah, I told you. It's best."

"I can't believe you. Every couple has issues."

"No, this is more than issues. This is dangerous ground we're treading. Something bad is going to happen; I can see it clearly."

It was time for my life to change. I didn't want to live that way anymore and I knew I had to stick to my decision and get out of there.

The dispatcher came on the line.

"Yes, I need a cab to pick me up at 335 W. Marathon Lane and take me to the bus station."

The dispatcher said the cab would be there in about fifteen minutes.

I was sitting at the foot of the bed, and Bre took her foot and kicked me in the back. She almost knocked me onto the floor.

I stood and looked at her with a look of disgust. "See, this is what I'm talking about. This right here is going to lead to something bad. I'm going to go wait outside."

I went to the front door and opened it, but the arguing commenced. I reached for my suitcase. She grabbed it and wouldn't let go. She tried to persuade me by crying, but my mind was made up. I knew her tears were an attempt to manipulate me into staying in what felt like hell, emotionally and mentally.

I stood there and began praying out loud. "God, help me please!" After praying with all my might, she stormed to the back.

I thought the iron was coming out, so I turned to walk out the door.

A young man with thick sandy blond hair wearing blue jeans and a pink dress shirt stood there with his back to me looking up at the sky.

I paused and looked at him. *Who was this? Where did he come from?* I wondered to myself. Then I noticed the cab. This man was the cab driver, but there was something about him that was kind of strange.

I walked out the door and stood next to him. He had on thin silver framed glasses and kept peering up into the sky.

"Hey, you're the cab driver, right?" I said.

At first, he didn't say anything. Then he looked at me with deep blue eyes behind those thin rimmed glasses. "Yes," he said, "and I have a message."

"A message? From who?"

"I have a message from God for Stacey."

I stood there looking at his eyes and started shaking uncontrollably.

He was about to say something when Bre came from the back and stormed to the front door. "Get your bags and go to the car."

I quickly did what he said. At the car, I put my bags in the trunk and got into the back seat.

I looked out the window and he and Bre were standing face to face. To this day, I have no idea what he said to her. But I do remember her face looking perplexed. Her eyes were so big. I didn't see her speak, and even though I was intoxicated, I will never forget the look on her face.

The young cab driver walked over to the car and got in. He turned to me. I sat in that back seat crying, smelling like Steel beer. But there was no judgment in his eyes, only comfort. "Give me your hands," he said.

I looked at his hands. They were so clean; there was not a bit of dirt under his nails. I slid my hands into his and he asked, "What's your name?"

"My name is Stacey."

"Jesus," he said as he began to pray for me. After he was done praying, he started driving.

I was free. I was finally going home where I belonged. I sat in the back sobbing. It was such a strange feeling. I felt happy, but I also felt a sense of loss and fear for what lay ahead.

When we arrived at the bus station, he asked me for my ticket. He got my bags out of the trunk and went and checked in my bags. Then he shook my hand and said, "Please be safe and blessed on your journey home."

With tears flowing down my face, I hugged him tight and said, "Thank you so much."

When he went back to his cab and got in, I remembered that I hadn't paid my cab fare, so I ran to him. "Hey! What's your name?"

He looked out his window. "My name is David."

"I forgot to pay you."

"No, when you get to your destination, make sure you go to church and put it in your tithe. Don't forget."

"I won't. I promise," I said.

Then he drove off. Gone, just like that.

The trip back home took a whole day. But I could hardly rest my head. I talked to God most of the way. I wasn't even sure if God wanted to hear from me. But I thought about what happened with David, and there was no question any longer in my mind that God intervened.

As I talked with God, I let him know that I wanted to change my life. I needed desperately for everything about my life to be different. I felt like I had traveled not only far from home, but so far from my heavenly father.

I was fearful to give up this persona that I had created in order to feel safe. But I knew it was time to give up my life for a life he wanted me to have and that it would take a miracle.

After all, I thought if God allowed all of that to happen to me, then I deserved it. That I had, somehow, asked for it. My thinking was so distorted. But still, I knew God was the only one I needed to turn to.

I wanted to trust in what I'd heard that his love could reach us no matter how far we'd gone. I prayed quietly in my heart, "God, please let your love reach me."

After hours of traveling, I was finally home. When I got off the bus, I literally fell on my knees and kissed the ground. My cousin Tony was there to pick me up and take me to the house.

That night, as I tried to go to sleep, I tossed and turned. I couldn't rest thinking about everything that happened.

I decided to get up and go to my mother's den. I put on worship music and lay face down on the floor. Suddenly, I felt a powerful presence in the room, and I knew it was God. As if I was watching a movie of my life, I saw the places I had been, people I was with and the things I had done. Without any warning, I heard this voice within me say, "Get up on your feet, now I'm going to make you into the woman I called you to be."

With tears pouring down my face, I stood on my feet. I felt so exhausted, so sleepy. All I could do was go back to bed, and I slept like I had not slept in years. The next morning, I knew something had changed in me. I knew God had met me that night and did a miracle in me. I had no desire to live my life outside of the will of God.

That morning, I committed my life to God, and I began to serve him. I served him for ten faithful years. I knew what my calling was, and I walked in it, and I loved every bit of it. I was finally experiencing freedom.

2 Corinthians 3:17 says, "Where the spirit of the Lord is, there is liberty." The freedom was so real, and I could only give God all the glory. But it was up to me to stay free.

Chapter Seven

Mercy

2016

I was so excited to have the opportunity to move to Delaware in order to help manage what was to become a chain of stores. I left everything I knew, my church, job, everything. I remember informing my former pastors of the move and they were gracious about it. They told me that I would know if I heard from God or not when I got there.

Although things did not work out the way I thought, I learned the truth of Romans 8:28, "ALL things work together for the good of them that love the Lord and called according to his purpose." I literally held on to that scripture for dear life.

The move resulted in so much disappointment for me. For some of it, I take the blame. I had false expectations and made some bad choices. I don't know what made me think that life wasn't going to happen in Delaware. When life hit me, I wasn't ready for it and I was hit with a strong blow.

I ended up becoming homeless, living out of my car. When this happened, I lost my balance. I fell off. There was still much work that needed to be done in me, still much that needed to be learned in order to stay sober.

One night, while living in my car, I couldn't take the pain anymore. I decided I deserved a drink. After all, I had gone all this time without one. *I can handle it,* I told myself. When discouragement outweighed the blessings and anger and resentment set in, I crumbled.

I honestly thought the first work was completed. But there was so much more transformation that needed to be done and the situation I found myself in proved that.

Once again, I found myself asking, "Why did I move here? Why did I leave everything I knew? What was I searching for?"

I went to get a six pack of beer, and then I sat in my car and drank one beer after the other and all the things that tormented me before came flooding back.

I felt so ashamed. *This time it's over. It's all over.* This thinking led me to go all the way. I was sure this was it. There was no way would God save me this time. But, once again, I was wrong. The word of God says in Jeremiah 33:11, "His mercy endures forever."

One morning, I sat in the parking lot of a movie theater crying. My soul was aching. Suddenly, God brought to my memory an 800 number I had stored into my phone from a pamphlet a co-worker had given me.

I called the number and a pleasant male voice answered. When I heard his voice, I almost hung up, but I didn't. "Hello," he said, "thank you for calling the addiction help line. How can we help you today?"

"Yes, I'm calling because I need help. I'm afraid I'm not going to make it another week. Please, help me." For the first time, I admitted that I had a substance problem. I suffered from alcoholism.

I explained to him that I was homeless, and my life had fallen apart. Instead of judging me, he said, "Well, you are in the right posture, a posture of surrender, true surrender."

This was actually the first time anyone had said that to me using that word *surrender.* It is such a powerful word.

He asked me for my health insurance card, but I had no idea where it was. I opened the dashboard and frantically pulled out all the papers. To my surprise, I found it. I gave him the information, but he became silent.   He wasn't aware of it, but I was mouthing the words, "Please, God. Please, God."

He said, "Ms. Stacey, we are going to help you. Can you stay by your phone? I'm going to have someone call you right back in three minutes. Please stay by your phone, ok?"

I mouthed the words, *Thank You Jesus!* and said, "Ok, I will."

It didn't take three minutes. Two minutes passed before the return call came.

This time, a young woman with a sweet voice said, "Ms. Stacey, we are going to help you. We would like to send you away to West Palm Beach, Florida, where your healing can begin. First, we will send you to a detox center where you'll spend five days and then to the treatment center from there. Would you be willing to do that?"

"Yes, absolutely," I said with a sigh of relief.

They provided me with a plane ticket for a flight the next day. May 24, 2016, was my last day drinking. The next day, I boarded a flight headed for Florida. I knew I was going to be facing some things in my life that I had never faced. I was putting my life in the hands of a bunch of strangers. Once again, I asked God to go with me and once again, he did.

Chapter Eight

Surrendered

I sat on the plane feeling extremely anxious. I kept adjusting my seat and looking back into the aisle. I couldn't keep still. Finally, the plane left the runway. Knowing I couldn't turn back brought me some sense of relief.

I calmed down and tried to sleep. When we landed, I was the last one off the plane. I said to God, "Well, this is it. I'm here. Now, you go with me, ok? Go all the way with me."

I headed straight to the baggage claim area. As I got closer, I noticed this man with a sign. It read John Doyle. That was the man they said would meet me at the airport once I landed.

I walked over and said hello.

"Hey there. Are you Stacey?"

"Yes, that's me."

With great enthusiasm, the man extended his hand to shake mine. "Well, now, it's a pleasure to meet you. Why don't you get your bags and we'll be on our way."

I was about to go somewhere I'd never been before with a total stranger but for some reason, the nervousness left me. It turned into excitement.

As I rushed over to get my bags, I started smiling. Something about this John guy felt familiar. I felt comfortable with him.

On the way to the detox center, he talked and talked. He talked about his addiction and shared his story of recovery.

I sat there thinking, *If everybody is like him, this is going to be a really interesting time to say the least.*

After about forty-five minutes, we arrived at the detox center. I got out of the van and watched John. With pep in his step, he grabbed my bags like he was a bellboy. He said, "Right this way, Ms. Stacey."

We entered a small corridor, and John rang a bell that was sitting outside a glass window. After a few minutes, a big, bald, giant guy came out. He had tattoos all over his arms and his head.

I looked at John with absolute terror; my face was all distorted.

John chuckled and said, "This is Rick. He's harmless. Rick, this is Ms. Stacey." My face started to relax as Rick extended his hand. "Good to meet you, Ms. Stacey. Right this way," he said.

He escorted me to an office where a few other staff members were located. Everyone stopped what they were doing and looked at me.

"Umm, hey everyone," I said feeling reluctant.

They all smiled and said, "Hello."

With a hand on my shoulder, John introduced me. "This is Ms. Stacey, everyone. She's going to be with us for the next five days."

I really didn't want his hand on my shoulder, but I knew his intent was to relax me so I didn't say anything.

The first thing they did was confiscate my cell phone. I said, "Oh, you need my phone?"

A young, freckled face redhead staffer named Becka said, "Yes, Ms. Stacey. For the five days that you're here, we want you to relax from the outside world and let us take care of you, ok?"

I nodded and said, "But I'm going to need it back when I leave."

She smiled and said, "Yes, ma'am."

After confiscating my phone and rambling through my things, I was escorted to the nurses station where my blood was taken. She asked if I wanted something for seizures or if I wanted to sign a waiver refusing the medication.

I thought to myself, *this is going to be a long five days cause I'm refusing this medication.* I said, "No, thank you. I want to go to bed. Where is my room?"

She finished her paperwork and said, "Right this way, Ms. Stacey."

They were a polite bunch. I didn't know whether to relax or be concerned, but I knew I was exhausted.

I was escorted to a neat, clean room. There was a flat screen TV mounted on the wall and feather filled pillows. I sat on the bed and said to myself, *this is it. I must be losing my mind. I've locked myself up on purpose.* But this wasn't Colorado Springs jail, this facility was plush. So, I lay down and it felt like I slept for the entire five days.

There, I met the sweetest, most honest people. People who were honest about their struggle, their addiction and their pain. There, we were all broken but determined to get unbroken. There, I experienced my first taste of what a recovery community was like.

After my five days there, I was transported to the treatment center. Me and another woman walked through those doors together and became roomies.

The treatment center was also plush. A chef cooked us three meals a day, and we had housekeeping and everything. I thought to myself, *you mean to tell me I had to have an addiction and lock myself up in order to be treated like a queen?* I chuckled at my own humor.

Again, I asked God to walk with me all the way. He took me by the hand and walked with me through the whole process of transformation.

In treatment, I learned the power of surrender. I gave up my power, the power I thought I had when I walked through those doors. I'm happy to share some of the things God used to strengthened me on the journey and help me get back up.

Chapter Nine

The Miracle

While I was in treatment, I began to face my feelings of inferiority, low self-esteem and worthlessness. I was able to see where the root of those things came from and with courage, I dealt with that root. In group counseling, my peers stood in for all those that had hurt me. They represented them and allowed me the opportunity to confront them and all that had hurt me.

I faced the rejection, abandonment and loss of identity in a safe place with people who truly wanted me to win and recover in every area of my life. I was surrounded by those who understood my struggle and why I could not stay clean and sober.

God used them to help save my life with honesty. There was no laying on of hands and no church sermons whatsoever. Now, don't get me wrong. We need the message of the Gospel. We need the body of Christ. We need the laying on of hands and prayer on our behalf.

But I learned that I needed to face the truth of what happened to me and not bury it inside while I was trying to help others or trying to hide behind church, ministry, the Bible or busyness. At the treatment center, they had me face the truth. The word of God says the truth will set you free (John 8:31, 32).

I've also learned that the journey truly is a process. In treatment, I was introduced to Alcoholics Anonymous. I met people like me. I really thought I was the only one with my story and the things that happened to me, but I was not. Listening to their stories blessed my soul; I could totally and absolutely identify. I could see the mercy of God through their story and my faith was renewed like never before.

I could feel my heart healing, I mean healing for real. I slowly began feeling a sense of confidence.

The shame was disappearing, and I began lifting my head.

I received my first book of Alcoholics Anonymous. At first, I was leery about reading this book. I didn't want it to conflict with my faith or with the word of God. But what I discovered when I decided to open it and read it was that much of what was in it was taken from Scripture.

I mean I could find a scripture for all twelve of the steps to recovery and I knew I was empowered even more so. I also learned that these twelve steps were not only for us in recovery. They are for everyone if everyone knew how to work them.

With the Gospel, the Word and recovery understanding, God empowered me. To this day, I feel more and more empowered every day as I live my life in recovery and in the Word.

When someone is intentional about the process in the journey, the twelve steps are basic biblical principles designed, if worked properly, to set an individual free.

I dove into that book. Along with my bible, I began to work the one on one and group counseling sessions. I completed personal projects and God began to do an amazing work in me and for me. Rather than an emotional experience this time around, it was intentional and intellectually infused.

I've learned that intellectual encounters with God are as important as emotional encounters with him. God not only wants to pull our hearts towards him, he wants to pull our minds towards him as well.

Romans 12:2 says, "Be transformed by the renewing of your mind." God was not only performing a miracle in my heart, he was also performing one in my mind. I began to see myself as a daughter and not an orphan.

The Lord began to open the doors so that my gifts could be used right there in treatment. The women there allowed me to pray with them and share Scripture with them that related to recovery using the AA book along with the Bible.

The facility even allowed me to hold a bible study in one of their conference rooms. Only God could have done that. He brought me back to life right there in treatment. This was God almighty showing himself to me like he had not shown me before. He was truly rescuing me, and I knew it.

Chapter Ten

The Rescue

The day finally came for me to leave. I knew upon my release I would need to take things a step further, so I decided to go live in a sober living environment. I lived there for three and a half years with other women in recovery. We laughed together, cried together and yes, even argued. But I would not trade the experience for anything.

Then God led me to my church. One day I attended an AA meeting and a sister there noticed I kept saying Jesus and quoting from Scripture but speaking on recovery. After the meeting, we got into a conversation, and she told me about a Christian recovery group at her church. I told her that I had been praying to God about something like that and I would like to go.

I was familiar with the church she was talking about. Every time I passed by this church, I said to myself that I was going to visit. I kept feeling drawn to this church whenever I passed by and here she was inviting to a Christian recovery group in this same church. This was truly the hand of God leading.

That Wednesday, I attended that faith-based group and listened to brothers and sisters who loved Jesus. Most attended the church faithfully. They had a joy. They weren't afraid to share their stories. They loved on one another, and it was real.

They spoke my language when it came to recovery (the intentionality of recovery, cooperating with God and partnering with him for healing and freedom). It felt like home. I started attending the church faithfully and getting connected to groups and ministries that matured me spiritually and my gifts began to flourish.

I have been sober for almost seven years, and I am still serving faithfully and helping other women recover, not only from substances but from all those things that leads us to the substance. The substance is only the manifestation of deeper issues.

I abandoned my persona that I created and being with women. My hope and prayer is that God will bring me my Amos. Yes, I smile saying that. It's an inside thing. God has restored my heart, mind and spirit and for that, I am eternally grateful.

God has shown me the importance and power of community, power in the love of community and the power in serving others. I am truly humbled by all that God has done. He chased me down every time and through his unfailing love and pursuit of me, he not only healed me, but he also rescued me. I am a RESCUED DAUGHTER!

About the Author

Stacey Winns grew up in the Bronx, New York, and currently resides in Virginia. She began writing poetry when she was fifteen years old. She has served in the recovery community for seven years helping others overcome addictions which are linked to false identity and negative behaviors. She also speaks publicly within the recovery world, encouraging a relationship with Jesus Christ and community.

Made in the USA
Columbia, SC
23 September 2024

42251808R00041